A thanksgiving sermon on the total repeal of the Stamp-act : preached in Cambridge, New-England, May 20th, in the afternoon preceding the public rejoicings of the evening upon that great occasion.

Nathaniel Appleton

Mr. *Appleton's*

SERMON

Occasioned by the Repeal

OF THE

STAMP-ACT.

A

Thankſgiving

SERMON

ON

THE TOTAL REPEAL

OF THE

STAMP-ACT.

PREACHED

In *Cambridge*, NEW-ENGLAND, *May* 20th,
in the Afternoon preceding the public Rejoicings of the Evening upon that great Occaſion.

By NATHANIEL APPLETON, M.A.
Paſtor of the Firſt Church in ſaid Town.

Publiſhed by the Deſire of the Audience, and at
theExpence of theHonorableBrigadierGeneral
BRATTLE.

The Lord hath done great Things for us, whereof we are glad.

*The Snare is broken, and we are eſcaped. Our Help is in the
Name of the Lord who made Heaven and Earth*
King DAVID

BOSTON
Printed and Sold by EDES and GILL, in Queen-
Street, 1766.

TO

THE RIGHT HONORABLE

WILLIAM PITT, ESQ;

All the Friends of Virtue,

AND

Patrons of Freedom,

Lovers of GREAT-BRITAIN,

And her Colonies;

Who have gloriously appeared in the Cause of

LIBERTY,

And obtained a Total Repeal of the

STAMP-ACT;

The following

DISCOURSE

Is most humbly and gratefully inscribed by

The AUTHOR.

A

Thanksgiving SERMON,

PSAL. XXX. 11, 12.

Thou haſt turned for me my mourning into danc-
ing. Thou haſt put off my ſackcloth, and girded
me with gladneſs To the end that my glory
may ſing praiſe to thee, and not be ſilent ; O
Lord my God, I will give thanks unto thee
forever.

THIS is a pſalm or ſong of praiſe to God,
composed (as the title of the pſalm expreſ-
ſes it) by David at the dedication of his
houſe But the pſalm is taken up in the
recounting the troubles and fears, difficulties and
dangers he had been in, and the merciful inter-
poſition of divine providence for his deliverance
out of them. And if we would have our hearts
truly and thoro'ly affected with divine goodneſs,
and our lips opened wide in devout praiſes to
God, we muſt look back to the troubles, the
fears, the dangers and diſtreſſes we have been in,
and from which God has delivered us For the
greatneſs of a mercy is according to the degree
of

of evil, miſery or calamity we are delivered from.
—This was the way by which the pſalmiſt's ſoul
was elevated in high devotion, his heart inlarged
in gratitude, and his lips opened wide in praiſe
to God —It ſhould ſeem he had not only been
under great difficulties and hazards, by his enemies, and by the hand of Saul, who from envy
and jealouſy ſought his life ; but that he had
been brought low, and upon the borders of the
grave by ſickneſs . But he cried unto the Lord,
and he heard him, and kept him alive that he
ſhould not go down into the pit , and he praiſes
God, that his anger endured for ſo little a while,
but for a moment, and then viſited with his
favour which is life *weeping endured for a night,
but joy came in the morning*, 5th v. of the context.
In the verſes of our text he obſerves, how wonderful the loving kindneſs of God had been to
him in this reſpect , that he had ſcattered the
clouds, changed the dark and gloomy ſcenes that
had been before him, and had opened ſuch new
ſcenes of joy and gladneſs as called for the
moſt enlarged gratitude and exalted praiſes.——
*Thou haſt turned for me my mourning into
dancing* · He went mourning becauſe of the
enemy and the oppreſſor, and was full of mourning becauſe of his ſickneſs, and the threatnings
of death · But now his mourning was turned
into dancing, his ſpirits were relieved of the
heavy burthen that lay upon them : and he felt
ſuch a lightneſs and chearfulneſs within upon his
deliverance,

deliverance, as inclined him to dancing and ſuch like tokens of joy. *Thou haſt put off my ſack-cloth* In times of trouble, and when under the mighty hand of God, by ſome ſore judgment or threatning evil, they were wont in token of humility to put on ſackcloth. Thus we find David and all the elders of Iſrael, in the time of the Lord's anger, and when threatned with deſtruction, clothed with ſackcloth.[*] But now God had put off his ſackcloth, had redreſſed his grievances, and removed his grounds of fear. *And guided me with gladneſs,* That is, ſo delivered him, ſo relieved and revived his ſpirit, as not only gave him peace and calmneſs of mind, but cauſed great joy and gladneſs of heart to him. *He guided him with gladneſs.* He compaſſed him about with gladneſs as with a girdle on every ſide. His ſoul was filled with joy and gladneſs appeared all about him, in his countenance, in his ſpeech, and in his whole behaviour. His troubles were removed, his burthens were taken off, his fears all vaniſhed, and ſo he was all joy and gladneſs. *To the end that my glory may ſing praiſe to thee, and not be ſilent.* That is, that his tongue might ſpeak and ſing the praiſes of God, and not ſuffer ſuch mercies to paſs in ſilence and without a due acknowledgment of them. God delivered him from all his troubles, and from all that was his fear, and guided him with gladneſs, with this view that David might ſee

B   the

[*] 1 Chron. 21. 16.

the power and goodneſs of God herein and celebrate his praiſes. *O Lord my God I will give*
thanks unto thee forever. He had ſuch a ſenſe
of the divine goodneſs, while he was thus girded
with gladneſs, that he was not only for ſinging
and ſpeaking forth the praiſes of God for the
preſent, but was for maintaining an abiding
ſenſe hereof upon his heart, ſo as ſhould be an
inexhauſtible fund for everlaſting praiſe. The
pſalmiſt had ſuch a ſtrong and lively ſenſe of the
ſalvations and deliverances he had of late receiv
ed, that it ſeemed to him that he ſhould never
forget the ſame But that the remembrance
hereof would be ſo freſh and ſtrong upon his
mind, that he ſhould feel an heart, and find a
tongue to celebrate his praiſes forever, and ever.

The words thus largely opened afford us the
following obſervations, which I hope will appear
ſeaſonable for our preſent meditation on the
great and glorious occaſion of our being this
day together in the houſe of God.——

1 OBS *The great God has the abſolute go-*
vernment of our affairs and circumſtances in
the world, and opens the various ſcenes of
life to us.

2 OBS. *It is the will of God, and what he*
has in view, when he changes the ſcene in
favour of his people, that they ſhould not
be ſilent, but ſhould awake their glory to
ſpeak and ſing his praiſe.

3. OBS.

3 OBS. *The true People of God desire to keep such a constant sense of the divine goodness as to be disposed to praise his name forever.*

1 OBS. *The great God has the absolute government of our affairs and circumstances in the world, and opens the various scenes of life to us.*

This is what we are taught in the text, and which is acknowledged to his glory. David passed thro' very various scenes of life, sometimes he was mourning in sackcloth · and then he was girded with gladness ; both which he ascribes to God. *Thou* hidest thy face and I was troubled, 7th v. *Thou* hast also girded me with gladness, as in the text. And this is a glorious character which God assumes to himself. *I even I am He and there is no God with me , I kill, and I make alive, I wound, and I heal, neither is there any that can deliver out of my hand**. *I form the light and create darkness , I make peace, and create evil I the Lord do all these things*†.——

Here let me say,

1st. *Whatever prosperous, afflicted or threatning circumstances we are at any time under, it is by the over-ruling providence of God.*

Shall there be any evil in the city, that is evil of affliction, and the Lord hath not done it ‡? Sometimes we are afflicted with bodily pains and sickness. " He is chastned with pain upon his bed, and the multitude of his bones with strong pain ;

* Deut 32 39   † Isaiah 45 7.   ‡ Amos 3 6.

his foul draweth near to the grave, and his life to the deftroyers"†. And he is ready to fay with Hezekiah when threatned with death by reafon of the difeafe that was upon him, " I faid in the cutting off my days I fhall go to the gates of the grave: I fhall not fee the Lord in the land of the living I fhali behold man no more with the inhabitants of the world He will cut me off with pining ficknefs"†. Sometimes God reduces to ftraits, poverty and famine . Sometimes he deprives of the deareft friends and relatives, and with them takes away the moft valuable enjoyments and the fweeteft comforts of life, and gives them to complain with the pfalmift, ? " Lover and friend haft thou put far from me, and mine acquaintance into darknefs.' Sometimes God hides the light of his countenance and they are troubled and while they fuffer God's terrors they are even diftracted. Sometimes God fo over-rules or permits it to be, that a people's rights and privileges are invaded, and infringed, they are greatly oppreffed, and bro't into flavery, or are under the fearful apprehenfion of it.   How did God over-rule as to his people Ifrael, that they fhould be fo many years in the land of Egypt, and in the houfe of bondage ? And how often did God afterwards, when fettled in their own land, for their finful departures from him, fell them into the hands of their enemies, who cruelly oppreffed them !

Sometimes

* Job 5, 17, 22   † Ifaiah 38. 10, 11, 12   ‡ 88 Pfalm 18

Sometimes such a severe hand was kept over them by those who had them in subjection, that they were not allowed, so much as a blacksmith in all Israel, lest they should make swords and spears, or any such weapons of defence, nor so much as their husbandry tools †. Or if a people are not actually brought into such a bondage as this, yet any approaches towards, or threatning such infringements, may well cause grief and fear, sorrow and mourning, in token of which they were wont in ancient time to put on sackcloth. Thus Mordecai clothed himself with sackcloth when that cruel edict of Ahasuerus came out against the Jews.*

And what a sorrowful, disturbed and tumultuous state have all the British colonies of America been in, when by a late parliamentary act, many of the privileges and liberties we had been in the quiet possession of, were cut short and should the act have continued, we should not have been the free people that once we were, and should have been subject to such oppressions as our fathers knew nothing of, and which neither we nor our children would have been able to bear

2dly. *Whenever the dark scene is changed, and a more agreeable one opens to us, it is God that does it for us.*

Thou hast turned for me, my mourning into dancing. *Thou* hast put off my sackcloth, and guided

† I Sam 13 19   * Eph 4 7, 3

girded me with gladneſs. That is, the great
God changes the ſcene, and gives us occaſion
for joy and gladneſs, and leads us to all the
natural outward expreſſions thereof.

Joy and ſorrow are human paſſions, and one or
the other is excited, according to the different
ſcenes God in his providence opens to us. Af-
flictions and fears, of themſelves, beget ſorrow
and mourning : But the removal of real afflic-
tions, ſcattering our fears, and putting us into
agreable circumſtances, begets a joy and gladneſs
of heart. And this joy is excited more or leſs
according or in proportion to the occaſion If
it be a ſore calamity, and a very grievous burden
we are delivered from, or if it be at ſuch a critical ſeaſon when the danger is imminent and
very threatning, and our fears run high ; remov-
ing ſuch a calamity, and ſcattering ſuch fears as
are gathering into diſtreſs and horror, creates ſo
much the greater joy and gladneſs And ſometimes the trouble, or the fear is ſo great and
preſſing upon the mind, that the ſudden removal
of the ſame excites a joy and gladneſs beyond
what we can expreſs : The ſalvation may be ſo
great, and ſo ſenſibly affect the mind, that men
of ſtrong paſſions, are ſometimes thrown into
rapturous extacies of joy —There is a joy unſpeakable and full of glory.

And how is God now turning our mourning
into dancing, putting off our ſackcloth and gird-
ing u. with gladneſs by the joyful and well
attested

atteſted news from that far, but mother country, which aſſures us that the grievous and bitter A C T which put us into mourning, covered us with ſackcloth, and threw us all into confuſion, is now REPEALED, *totally repealed*, made null and void, by the KING, LORDS, and COMMONS, in parliament aſſembled; ſo as to be as if it had never been!

Oh! with what joy and gladneſs does it gird every true-born Engliſhman, every friend to liberty, and every true lover of his country, his mother country or theſe Britiſh colonies! what joy does now fill every breaſt, what gladneſs appears in every face and feature! and how does every one feel himſelf ready to burſt forth in loud acclamations of joy!

But to exhilerate your ſpirits, and excite your joys in a rational manner, and as becomes men of thought and judgment, who would always govern this very paſſion of the ſoul by ſolid and ſubſtantial reaſon; I ſay, in order to this, let us only conſider the deplorable condition the nation and all theſe colonies muſt have been in, if the government at home had eſtabliſhed the ACT, and proceeded to the inforcement of the ſame. If theſe had been the heavy tidings from home, that the parliament inſiſted upon the rigorous execution of this *act* in all the American plantations, and that in order to it *fleets* were forming, *forces* raiſing, and a grand armament preparing, to inforce obedience to the ACT. I ſay if theſe had been the doleful tidings, Oh what grief, what fear, what conſternation, and confuſion, ſhould we have been put into ! what anger and wrath, what reſolution, what oppoſition, what force, what violence would this irritated people have gone into ! what deſolation, what ſlaughter, and bloodſhed might have been expected !———And what an unſpeakable hurt muſt it have brought upon us, and upon our mother country ! what an alienation of affection, what an interruption of mutual trade and commerce deſtructive to them as well as to us !

Moreover, How would they and we be expoſed to our watchful and perfidious enemies, who would ſuddenly and eagerly have catch'd at ſuch a favourable opportunity to make repriſals upon us !———

Surely when we conſider the very extenſive as well as pernicious influence of this ACT, how deeply it would affect the nation as well as the colonies and what contention and ill blood, yea, what violence, and ſhedding of blood, what deſtruction, and deſolation is happily prevented by the repeal of this act. Every one who loves his neighbour, who is concerned for the public peace and ſafety, or that has any humanity, or bowels of compaſſion, muſt be glad and rejoice at this merciful deliverance

But then by the repeal of this oppreſſive act, there is a poſitive good accruing, that may ſerve

furthe·

further to excite the joy, and increaſe the gladneſs of our hearts. This ſerves to indear the KING (if poſſible) yet more and more to us, and fill us with gratitude as well as loyalty to him, and to his royal houſe, and will induce this people with all freedom to ſacrifice their very lives and fortunes for the ſupport and defence of his crown and dignity

This alſo will maintain within us a juſt honor for, and dutiful regard to the Britiſh parliament, as the ſupreme legiſlative power of the nation, who heard our cauſe and redreſſed our grievances.

This alſo will fix upon our hearts a moſt grateful remembrance of thoſe wiſe and worthy patriots, who heartily eſpouſed and ſo ſtrenuouſly pleaded our cauſe, and ſet things in ſo clear and convincing a light, as to procure the repeal of ſuch a diſagreable and deſtructive act. Theſe great and good men, I ſay, who have exerted themſelves according to their ſuperior abilities, and their inviolable attachment to juſtice, truth and liberty in our behalf, will be remembred with honor, love and gratitude, and their memory bleſſed we hope in future generations.

Moreover, by reaſon of this happy repeal, love and affection between the mother country and us, will return with its wonted ardor Commerce and trade will be carried on with the former freedom, to the mutual advantage of both them and us And we ſhall be ready upon every

C   occaſion,

occasion to strengthen one another's hands for mutual safety against the common enemy. And it gives the most pleasing prospect of the growing greatness of the British empire. So that all who love the peace and prosperity of the nation and all its dependencies, and are pleased to see so sweet and pleasant a thing as brethren dwelling together in unity and love; must needs rejoice and be exceeding glad at this happy turn of times, as one of the most distinguishing and extensive blessings of an outward nature that we ever received.

2 OBS. *It is the will of God, and what he has in view, when he changes the scene in favour of his people, that they should not be silent, but should awake their glory to speak and sing his praise.*

To the end that my glory may sing praise to thee and not be silent. The great God will have us not only glad and joyful for any agreable and happy turn of affairs; but would have us also thankful. Many people are glad at the good news, and agreable change of affairs; but not thankful. They feel a pleasing sensation within, but no due sense of God, or religious acknowledgment of him. Whereas, this is what God expects and requires of us as men, and christians. *He girds me with gladness, to the end that my glory may sing praise to him, and not be silent.*

By the psalmist's glory some understand his *soul,* his rational and intellective powers, which
are

ate indeed the glory of the man. But others underſtand it rather of his *tongue*, as *ſinging* and
not keeping ſilence mentioned in the text are
appropriate to the tongue.

Let us take them together; reaſon, religion
and ſpeech are the diſtinguiſhing glory of man
above every creature upon the footſtool. and
this glory taking it collectively, is not to be *ſilent*
when we receive any ſignal favours from God;
but to ſhew forth his praiſe. *Reaſon* is to conſider the greatneſs of benefits received, with all
the great and happy conſequences thereof. *Religion* is to view the great God as the author, and
giver of every good thing, and to obſerve the
great and the undeſerved goodneſs of God, in
all the merciful and powerful interpoſitions of
his providence, and the tongue is to ſpeak and
ſing, and thereby to ſhew forth the praiſes of God.

And who will ſuffer his glory to be ſilent?
who can refrain from meditating upon the great
and wonderful things God has done for us, and
from having his heart enlarged in thankfulneſs,
and his mouth filled with praiſes? Surely reaſon,
and religion, and the tongue, ſhould all awake
upon this great and joyful occaſion, and not be
ſilent

We ſhould ſet our *reaſon* to work, and conſider the greatneſs, extenſiveneſs, and vaſt importance of the affair for which we are at this time
celebrating the praiſes of God.

The

The *Stamp Act* was very exten{ive, not only as to the va{t variety of articles contained in it; but as to tho{e who were {ubjected to it, and would be very much affected by it. It extended to all the Briti{h {ubjects in America, from Canada to Florida, comprehending all the Briti{h I{lands. Moreover, our rea{on and judgment tells us, that it greatly affected Great Britain it{elf in all its merchandize and manufacture and indeed that the whole Briti{h empire would have felt the ill influence of it and con{equently that the repeal of this act has relieved a multitude of people, and filled many thou{ands and millions with joy. For rea{on tells us this is the mo{t effectual method of preventing any grievous breach between the mother country, and the{e her colonies, and of pre{erving the peace, love, and happy harmony that have {o long {ub{i{ted between us, and of e{tabli{hing the power, wealth and pro{perity of all. And {o in {hort rea{on tells us, that this is one of the greate{t affairs, as to its influence and con{equences, that has been tran{acted in the nation for many ages. I believe it will be readily yielded, that there has {carcely been one thing of {o great importance to the Briti{h nation and colonies, {ince the *happy revolution* near four{core years ago, by King William of glorious memory, as the total repeal of the {tamp act.

Now let religion {peak, and let us {et our{elves con{ider that divine power and influence by
which

which this happy repeal has been effected ——— Religion teaches us to view the hand of God in every thing. Religion teaches us that by the divine permiſſion that oppreſſive act was paſs'd, by which God hid his face from us, teſtified his anger, and let us ſee what our ſins deſerved: and that it is of his undeſerved mercy, and thro' his all governing influence, that it is now repealed.

We may ſee, and we ought to obſerve, ſo far as we can, the natural means by which things are brought about ; but we muſt look above and beyond all human means and natural cauſes, to him *who fitteth upon the circle of the earth*, and who guides and governs in univerſal nature.

We may ſee, and we ought with gratitude to obſerve, the wiſdom, the ſagacity, the faithfulneſs, the indefatigableneſs of our generous friends in eſpouſing and ſolliciting our cauſe ; and we may ſee the various arguments made uſe of, and the happy influence they had upon the King, and Parliament But we muſt look thro' all theſe to the great Governor of the world, who has the hearts of Kings, and of all men in his own hands, to change and turn them even as the rivers of water are turned: and ſo religion ſees the hand of God in bringing about this repeal. And the good chriſtian will trace the foot-ſteps of divine providence, ſo far as is plain and obvious, and where it is beyond his penetration, he will conſider it as the work of the Lord, and regard it as the operation of his hands Thus the chriſ-

tian

tian obſerves the hand of God in that general commotion ſtirred up in the nation when the act was firſt paſſed, and the time of its taking place appointed. The providence of God is alſo to be ſeen in the univerſal uneaſineſs and clamour in all the colonies upon the firſt tidings of it, all as one man riſing up in oppoſition to it; ſuch a union as was never before ſeen in all the colonies.

Moreover, God is to be ſeen in the change of the miniſtry at ſuch a critical and important ſeaſon, and calling ſuch eminently worthy patriots into the adminiſtration, who ſaw the dreadful conſequences of inforcing the ſtamp act, and were (as we underſtand) to a man for the repealing it. And how viſible is the hand of God in raiſing up ſuch wiſe, able and faithful, friends and advocates to ſollicit the repeal, and in filling their mouths with ſuch clear, ſtrong and cogent arguments, to convince and perſwade of the abſolute neceſſity of a total repeal. Such as the Duke of Grafton, Marquiſs of Rockingham, Lord Dartmouth, Lord Camden, General Conway, the right Honorable William Dowdeſwell, Eſq, Sir William Meredith, Sir George Saville, Col Barre, great and worthy patriots, whom God has raiſed up and honoured as eminent inſtruments of our deliverance. And how viſible is the hand of God, more eſpecially with reſpect to the great, the good, and the excellent Mr Pitt, that grand patron of true virtue, and of Engliſh liberty.

and

and whom God has once and again raised up to be the deliverer of these British colonies from captivity, and slavery I say, how remarkable was the kind hand of providence, that notwithstanding his chronical grievous malady of body, his soul was inspired with such a sacred ardor for his country's safety, that he surmounted all the difficulties of bodily pain and weakness, and appeared in that august assembly with all his flannels, and was enabled to utter himself with such clearness, closeness, plainness and faithfulness as carried conviction with it, and had its desired effect. Religion teaches us that the greatGod made so great a man, formed and fitted him for such eminent services, and used and honored him as such a public Saviour to the British Israel.

Moreover, Religion teaches us to see the great God standing in the congregation of the mighty, and judging among the Gods, presiding both in the house of Commons, and in the house of Lords, exciting their attention to the weighty reasonings, and causing them to feel such force and energy therein, as to change their mind, and be inclined to repeal what they so lately enacted, being convinced this was the best if not the only way to save the nation and its colonies from ruin. Now that majority of Parliament is to be highly honored, for their regard to the public good, that they no sooner saw the dangerous tendency of their late act, but they speedily made it null and void. But as we would honor

nor and re∫pect every man, that has given his
hand or voice for the public ∫afety; ∫o we would
∫ee the hand of God in all this remarkable event,
from the beginning to the end For religion
will not allow us to attribute any thing to meer
chance, but points out the hand of God in the
mo∫t ca∫ual events.   In what is there more chance
than in votes, and lots? But what ∫ays the wi∫e
man? Prov. 16. 33. *The lot is ca∫t into the lap,
but the whole determination is of the Lord.*

Well now, when rea∫on and religion teach us
the∫e things, what is the tongue, that glory of
men to do upon it? Why be ∫ure, not to be *∫ilent*,
but to awake and talk of all his wondrous works,
to ∫ing unto him, and to give prai∫e.

And who will,   or who can ∫uffer his
glory to be ∫ilent, or refrain from ∫hewing forth
the prai∫es of God for this remarkable glorious
in∫tance of his goodnes and mercy? O! how
∫hould our lips be opened in the mo∫t exalted
prai∫es of God, and ∫ay he is our God and we
will prai∫e him, our father's God and we will
prepare him an habitation, who has remembred
us in our low e∫tate, and in the critical hour gave
the vote for us! What prai∫es are due to almighty
God from this people? that he gave us favour
in the eyes of the King and of his Mini∫try, and
of his Lords and of his Commons, who have
redre∫∫ed our grievances, and taken away the
heavy yoke, that neither we nor our children
would have been able to bear, whereby he has
                                        relieved

relieved our diſtreſſed minds, removed the gloom that hung upon every face, turned our mourning into dancing, put off our ſackcloth, and girded us with gladneſs. Oh! how then ſhould we *praiſe him with joyful lips, and ſhew forth his praiſe from day to day? I will bleſs the Lord at all times, his praiſe ſhall continually be in my mouth. My ſoul ſhall make her boaſt in the Lord, the humble ſhall hear thereof, and ſhall be glad. O! magnify the Lord with me, and let us exalt his name together, and ſay, bleſs the Lord O our ſouls, and forget not all his benefits · Our ſoul is eſcaped as a bird out of the ſnare of the fowler, the ſnare is broken, and we are eſcaped, our help is in the name of the Lord who made heaven and earth.*

But then we muſt employ our tongue, our glory, not only to ſpeak but to ſing his praiſes. This is the language of gratitude and true devotion, *O come let us ſing unto the Lord, let us make a joyful noiſe to the rock of our ſalvation.*

Moreover we find in Ezra's day*, that the people in praiſing the Lord ſhouted with a great ſhout. *Be glad then in the Lord, and rejoice ye righteous, and ſhout for joy all ye that are upright in heart*

3 Obs. *The true people of God deſire to keep up ſuch a conſtant ſenſe of divine goodneſs, as to be always diſpoſed to praiſe his name, and to give thanks to him forever.*

D

O

* Ezek 3 11.

O Lord my God ! I will give thanks unto thee forever. A truly grateful people will not content themſelves with a few thankful acknowledgments, or in attending the public worſhip of God in a way of praiſe and thankſgiving for an hour or two, or in bonfires and illuminations the evening after ; but will labour to retain a grateful ſenſe of divine favours all their life long, and to tranſmit the memory of God's great goodneſs to future generations.   This will be the care of a godly and a grateful people, not to forget any of God's benefits ; eſpecially ſuch as are public, remarkable and very important ; but to preſerve the memory of them from generation to generation. *We will not hide them from their children, ſhewing to the generations to come the praiſes of the Lord, and his ſtrength and his wonderful works which he hath done , that the generations to come might know them, even the children which ſhould be born, who ſhould ariſe and declare them to their children, that they might ſet their hope in God, and not forget the works of God, but keep his commandments* .

Thus the grateful and the gracious ſoul will be for giving thanks to God forever in this world, as he will endeavour that one generation ſhall praiſe his works to another, and declare his mighty acts   But then the pious thankful ſoul will praiſe this God forever and ever, in the other world, where all the wonders of divine goodneſs,

* Pſal. 78. 4 6 7.

goodnefs, and all his feafonable appearances for his church and people will fo open themfelves to the faints, as to fill them with new matter of admiration and praife to all eternity.

How careful fhould we then be to perpe-tuate the memory of this late fignal deliverance: and endeavour that God may be praifed forever and ever upon the account hereof: and when we are fleeping in the duft of *death* which can-not praife God, and in the *grave* which cannot celebrate him, our children may rife up and praife him; and fo from generation to generation. And we wifh to God there may be fuch lafting, happy and bleffed effects of this repeal, as to our religious as well as civil interefts, as that we and our children may have occafion for rendering everlafting praifes to God in heaven. And if the repeal of this act fhould be the means of con-tinuing our religious as well as civil liberties, and of tranfmitting pure and undefiled religion to future ages Oh ! what a refource will it be of perpetual and everlafting praifes !

But then, as we are to keep up a grateful per-petual remembrance of God's great mercy to us, that fo we might praife him forever and ever, fo it becomes us to keep up a continued grateful re-membrance of thofe worthy honorable patriots whom God has made eminent inftruments of good unto us. Ingratitude to friends and bene-factors is to be abhorred · and if we would not be ungrateful, we may not be forgetful of fuch

who

who have been diftinguifhingly kind, and good
to us   But muft endeavour to perpetuate their
names with honor . that they who rife up after
them, and us, may call them bleffed.   The memory of the juft is bleffed   and the righteous
fhall be had in everlafting remembrance   And
it is highly juft and reafonable, that they who
have received fpecial benefits from the great and
the good, fhould do their part that the memory
of fuch may be bleffed.

And as God has in this late dark day, and critical juncture, raifed up powerful friends, and
worthy benefactors to us, who by their wifdom
and zeal, their courage, conftancy and clofe ap-
plication in our behalf, have procured this glorious deliverance for us , furely we can do no
lefs than call them bleffed, by wifhing bleffings
of every kind to them and theirs   and not only
fo, but fhould endeavor that the memory of
their good deeds may be handed down with honor, not only in the annals of time and hiftory
of the prefent age , but by fome lafting monu-
ment or other

And if it was in our power, how agreable
would it be to have the glorious Mr. Pitt, and
others of the fore mentioned Worthies, who are
avowed enemies of corruption, tyranny and op-
preffion, who are the faft friends of virtue, and
powerful advocates for liberty , at the fame time
lovers of their king, their nation, and all the
colonies . I fay, how agreable would it be to
have

have brazen or marble monuments erected, not only to perpetuate their memory, but to let the future ages see the truly grateful sense we had of their patriotic goodness in the time of it? I don't mean idolatrous images, to fall down and worship, which was the superstition and folly of the ancient heathen, with respect to their heroes ; but to present to future ages the resemblances of such whom God formed, raised up, and made such eminent instruments of saving the British Empire from impending ruin.

All that I have further to add here is, that in our praises and thanksgivings to God for this present merciful deliverance, we join our humble fervent prayers that this our tranquility may be lengthened out to future generations, and that this people may never more be molested in such a manner: But that we and ours may be continued in the quiet possession of all our constitutional rights from age to age. And as the God of our fathers has so wonderfully appeared for us at this time, we may confidently hope and trust he will for time to come, if we walk in his ways, and serve him with a perfect heart and a willing mind. And indeed considering, how fully this affair was debated in parliament, and the judgment of some eminently learned in the law, of both houses of parliament relative to constitutional right,* and taking many other things

* It appears by the public prints that Lord Camden in the house of Lords and Mr Pitt in the House of Commons, declared the Stamp Act to be unconstitutional

things into conſideration, we have no ground to fear any thing of this ſort, ſo long as we approve ourſelves loyal ſubjects of king George, and his ſucceſſors in the Britiſh throne, and yield all due ſubjection to the Britiſh Parliament.

And, as the Jews of old, when they were de-livered from the cruel edict of the king for their deſtruction, were filled with gladneſs and praiſe, and kept up an anniverſary ſolemnity in joyful remembrance of their deliverance, which was a *day of gladneſs and feaſting, a good day, and of ſending portions one to another*|. So now ſince this parliamentary edict which alarmed all our fears, and filled us with diſtreſs, is abſolutely and entirely repealed, let every one be girded with gladneſs, and every tongue ſing praiſe to God.

And as this religious exerciſe will be followed with public rejoicings, and external tokens of joy, let me earneſtly exhort you all, both old and young, high and low, to conduct with all that decency & due decorum, which becomes thoſe who have been in the houſe of God this day, pouring out our devout religious acknowledgments before him; and attending upon the counſels of his word. Let me intreat you, and in the name and fear of God, let me charge you in all your mirth to refrain from every thing that is *profane*, from every thing that is *rude* or *unſeemly*, from every thing that is *intemperate* and contrary to the rules of ſobriety, and from every thing that

is

† Eſtta 9 19.

is *miſchievous* or hurtful to the perſons or pro-
perties of others.

And let me further caution you againſt ma-
naging your rejoicing in a way of triumph or
inſult upon any perſons at home (for I know of
none among ourſelves) who have appeared zea-
lous promoters of the act which is now aboliſh-
ed. And that you avoid every thing that is ir-
ritating or provoking to mens ſpirits, or that
tends to beget ill-will. For we know of no man,
but whoſe help and good-will we may ſometime
or other have occaſion for. Finally here let me
adviſe you to break up your diverſions in good
ſeaſon, and return every one quietly to his place
of abode · And may every thing be conducted
with ſo good order, and with ſuch innocency of
behaviour as becomes the diſciples of Chriſt, who
joy in the Lord, and when they greatly rejoice,
it is in the God of their ſalvation. And if theſe
external rejoicings flow from, or are accompanied
with true gratitude to the God of heaven, who
has appeared for our help, it will be a token of
farther good.

Let me add one word more and have done ;
and that is, that we *pay all due reſpect to the
civil magiſtrate*, and a willing ſubjection to the
government over us, whether ſupreme or ſubor-
dinate. Let us conſider the true deſign of government, which is the *good of the community* ;
and fixing this in our mind as a firm principle,
it will ſerve very much to direct, and regulate as

to all exertions of power, as well as to our obedience and ſubmiſſion thereunto. I ſhall re-
commend to you the apoſtolic advice, 1 Pet. 2.
13—17. *Submit yourſelves to every ordinance of*
man for the Lord's ſake, that is, to every conſti-
tutional ordinance of man that is not repugnant
to the ſuperior law of God and nature, *whether*
it be to the King as ſupreme, or unto governors,
as unto them that are ſent by him, for the puniſh-
ment of evil doers, and for the praiſe of them that
do well For ſo is the will of God, that with
well doing ye may put to ſilence the ignorance of
fooliſh men As free, and not uſing your liberty
for a cloke of maliciouſneſs, but as the ſervants
of God. Honor all men, love the brotherhood
fear God and honor the King. PRAYING al-
ways for Kings, and for all in authority, and that
you yourſelves may lead quiet and peaceable lives
in all godlineſs and honeſty.

And now bleſſed be the Lord who hath done
great things for us, whereof we are glad Bleſſed
be the Lord God, the God of Iſrael, who *only*
doth wondrous things, and bleſſed be his glorious name forever, and let the whole earth be
filled with his glory. AMEN, and AMEN

CPSIA information can be obtained
at www.ICGtesting.com
Printed in the USA
BVHW061113100220
571921BV00016B/449

9 781275 828445